"This is the best field trip ever."

Marcus tiptoed to the center of the court.

Bright lights suddenly beamed down on the court. Marcus knew that was his moment to shine. He quickly lifted his hands high in the air. His hands were grasping the ball he was saving for Jason Carter. Then Marcus imagined the crowd screaming his name. He raised up on the balls of his feet and stretched his body toward the basket. Just as Marcus was about to shoot the ball, he heard thundering footsteps.

"Who is that on my playground, ground, ground...?" a hollow voice cried out and echoed into the bleachers.

The deep voice startled the kids. Marcus wobbled on his tiptoes as he stood in perfect position to release his shot.

THE REAL SLAM DUNK

by **Charisse K. Richardson**

illustrated by **Kadir Nelson**

 HOUGHTON MIFFLIN

BOSTON

ACKNOWLEDGMENTS

With special gratitude to Teresa Artis-Richardson, Kathy Behrens, Kevin Carr, Angernett Carter, Cheryl Day, Henry Hicks, Billy Holliday, Todd Jacobson, Adrienne Lotson, Steven Neville, Charly Palmer, Camilla Ratliff, Bernice Richardson, Derrick Stafford, Dorothea Taylor, Jennifer C. Thomas, and Mardi Woods. Also a world of thanks to Michael Carlisle, R. Diane Gedymin, and Angelle Pilkington for believing in the possibilities!

Printed in China

ISBN-13: 978-0-618-93266-5
ISBN-10: 0-618-93266-6

1 2 3 4 5 6 7 8 9 SDP 15 14 13 12 11 10 09 08

To D.R., who made my dream our dream,
and to Christopher, always know that
you can be anything you want to be!
—C.K.R.

CHAPTER 1

Boom! The front door slammed so hard the house shook.

"Oops!" Marcus whispered, freezing in his tracks.

"Marcus Trey Robinson!" his mother yelled.

"Hi, Mom! Sorry about the door," he said. He wished he could remember that his mother hated when he slammed the door. "It's just that tomorrow is the big day!"

"For what?" his mom asked.

"The field trip!" Mia, Marcus's twin sister, blurted as she rushed into the kitchen. She had a round face with bushy eyebrows, just like Marcus. She plopped her backpack on the kitchen table.

"Tomorrow we go to Giants Practice Day," Marcus reminded his mother.

A smile blossomed on her face. "Oh, that's right. You get to meet what's-his-name," his mom said jokingly.

"Mom! His name is Jason Carter. You know...Jasooon Carterrr!" Marcus stretched the name out like the announcers on TV did.

"Everybody knows who Jason Carter is," Mia said as she grabbed the glue and scissors from a drawer. Then she sat down at the table and began cutting out pictures of basketballs from a magazine. She was going to paste the basketballs next to the story about

Jason Carter she was writing for her newspaper. Mia's "newspaper" was really just a poster board filled with pictures and stories she made up and typed on the computer. She kept telling Marcus that one day it would be as big as the *City News Times*—that was the newspaper their parents read.

"I know who Jason Carter is," their mom said with a laugh. "How could I forget?"

Marcus's room breathed Jason Carter. Basketball posters of him were tacked up all over his walls. If he got any more, he would have to paste them to the ceiling.

"You know your father wishes he were in your class. He wants to go on the field trip, too," she told them.

Marcus was too excited to stand still. He did an air dribble. Then he turned and stretched his arms high above his head.

As he leaped toward the refrigerator, his

mom screamed, "Marcus Robinson hits the winning basket!"

"Mom, I was in the middle of my shot," he groaned. "You made me miss it."

"Even Jason Carter misses baskets," his mom said with a laugh.

Marcus pointed at the front of his Jason Carter jersey. "Number Fourteen hardly ever misses," he said.

"Are you wearing that smelly shirt again tomorrow?" Mia asked. She fanned her hand up and down in front of her nose.

"Of course I am," Marcus said. His Jason Carter jersey was his favorite. It had been too big when he got it a few years ago. Now it was almost too small. But he loved it so much, he wouldn't give it up. His mom usually didn't let him wear it two days in a row. Since they were going on the field trip, he hoped she would say it was okay.

Marcus crossed his fingers behind his back and looked up at his mother.

Please say yes, he begged silently.

"If you wash it, you can wear it tomorrow," his mom said.

"Yeeeessss!" Marcus yelled. Then he hunched back over and began air dribbling again.

"Make this your last shot," his mom said. "It's time to do homework."

Marcus stood straight up and sighed. "Aw, Mom, homework is such a waste of time," he said. It wasn't that school was hard. Marcus secretly loved math. He just didn't think he'd ever use what he learned in school. He was only ten, but he already had his mind made up. He was going to be a famous basketball player one day—just like Jason Carter.

"You can't bounce your way into college," his mom said.

"But, Mom, I know I'm good," he said. "I'm the best! That's why I was named Most Valuable Player for our team last season."

"Okay, hotshot," she said. "One more shot. Then dribble your way to the kitchen table to do your homework until your dad gets home."

Marcus prepared to make a slam dunk. He quietly lifted his arms in the air and aimed for the top of the refrigerator.

Mia walked past him and grabbed a frozen strawberry juice bar from the freezer. Her eyes met the hair on top of his bushy head.

Marcus had refused to get a haircut for the last four weeks. He thought he would look taller if he let his hair grow. But it wasn't working. Mia was still almost an inch taller.

Marcus walked to the table and unzipped his backpack. He noticed lying on the table there was a picture of Jason Carter that Mia had clipped from a magazine. Marcus picked up the picture and stared at Jason.

"Everyone has signed the basketball we're giving to Jason," Mia told Marcus between slurps. "Now all I need is the tape recorder so I won't miss anything Jason says." She wanted to write a story about what Jason was going to tell them. The tape recorder would help her remember exactly what he said.

Marcus put the picture back on the table. Then he pulled a notebook from his backpack. "Don't forget I'm the one who gets to ask Jason the questions," he said. Marcus wondered if Jason would find out Mia was his twin—especially since she was a smidgen taller than he was. He thought that would be too embarrassing. Maybe if he stayed far away from her, Jason would never notice.

Just as Marcus sat down, his father opened the front door.

"Hey, Dad," Marcus shouted, jumping up

and running to meet him. "Guess what I'm going to ask Jason Carter tomorrow?"

"You can tell me when we get in the car," his dad said, patting the top of Marcus's head. "We're off to the barbershop."

Marcus sighed. "Do I *have* to get a haircut?"

"You sure do," his father said.

Marcus's mom kissed his dad hello. Then she looked at his hair. "*You* could use a haircut, too," she told her husband. "But hurry back. Marcus still has homework to do."

CHAPTER 2

Marcus woke up early the next morning, even before his alarm clock rang. He rubbed his eyes and peeked over the side of his bed. His Fly Carter sneakers stared up at him. They were right where Marcus had left them. He could hardly wait to put them on.

Marcus quickly got dressed and laced up his shoes. Then he rushed out of his room. He forgot about his haircut until he caught a glimpse of himself in the hallway mirror. He stopped and stared. He looked closer and closer, searching for hair on his head. But mostly he saw scalp. He moaned.

Then Marcus raced down to the laundry room to get his jersey. He had tossed it in the dryer the night before with two fabric softener sheets. His mom always used those to make the clothes smell nice. It was the first time Marcus had put the jersey in the dryer. His mom usually washed it in the sink and hung it to dry. But Marcus wanted it to smell extra fresh for the field trip.

Marcus smiled as he yanked his jersey out of the dryer and inspected it.

"Oh no!" he shrieked. His eyes nearly popped out of their sockets.

"What happened?" Mia asked, running down the stairs.

Their mom was a few steps behind. She

leaped down the stairs two at a time.

Marcus stood there frozen. The crumpled jersey hung from his fingers. It had shrunk to half its original size. It looked as if it wouldn't fit even a skinny five-year-old.

"What am I going to do?" he cried.

"I'm so sorry," his mother said. "I'm sure there is something else you can wear that will look just fine. At least you have on your Fly Carter sneakers." Then she bent down and gave him a warm hug.

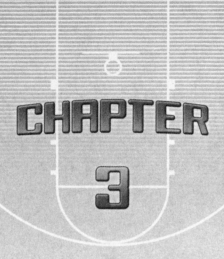

CHAPTER 3

"Why aren't you wearing your jersey, Marcus?"

"What happened to your hair?"

That was all Marcus heard that day at school.

Juan was the only person he told about his jersey. They had been best friends since pre-school. Marcus knew Juan would understand.

"But you're his biggest fan. You have to

wear a Jason Carter jersey," Juan told him at lunch. "And you are the official greeter for our class," he added, stuffing his hot dog in his mouth. A drop of ketchup splattered on the Jason Carter jersey he was wearing.

Juan looked down at his shirt and frowned.

"I know," Marcus said, pushing the plate with his half-eaten hot dog away.

Marcus had won the math competition at school the week before. His prize made him the envy of the whole school. He got to be the official greeter on their field trip to see Jason Carter and the Giants.

The class always got to decide the prize before each math contest. There were all kinds of goodies to choose from—a baseball jersey, a glow-in-the-dark yo-yo, circus tickets, and passes to the zoo. Marcus usually thought the prizes were boring.

Then last week Mia had a fantastic idea. "What if the next winner gets to be the greeter for our field trip?" she asked. "They can ask Jason most of our questions."

"What a marvelous idea!" Ms. Jordan said. "The winner of Friday's math contest will be the official greeter for our class next week."

Marcus thought that was the best idea his sister had ever had. He studied so hard his eyelids burned. And it showed. He didn't miss a single question in the contest.

And Ms. Jordan surprised him with an extra prize. She pulled a brand-new basketball from under her desk. She said the whole class would get to sign the ball, and Marcus would present it as their gift to Jason Carter.

• • •

Brring, Brring! The bell rang.

"School's out!" Marcus shouted. At first, he

tore down the hall like a rocket. But when he
remembered that he was missing his jersey,
he slowed down.

"Wait up, Marcus!" Mia shouted.

Rupert passed them in the hallway. He
was always stirring up trouble. "I thought
you guys were twins," Rupert said, looking
back at them.

"We are!" Mia said, glaring at him.

"Then how come Marcus is shorter than you?" Rupert teased. And he took off running.

Rupert's words echoed in Marcus's ears. Marcus dropped his head and suddenly wished he could melt into the floor.

They finally reached the school bus. Someone had written the word GIANTS in big letters in the dirt on the side of the bus.

"One Practice Day ticket for you, and one ticket for you," Ms. Jordan told the twins as they hopped on board.

Marcus carefully tucked his ticket into his jeans pocket. He didn't want to lose it like he sometimes did with his lunch money.

As Marcus made his way down the narrow aisle, someone shouted out to him, "Don't forget to ask him my question!"

"Yeah. Remember what I said to ask him," someone else yelled.

"You better not forget to ask mine," Rupert snapped.

"We'll see," Marcus said, sneering back at him.

"Over here," Juan said, patting the empty spot next to him.

Marcus slid into the seat. He gave Juan a weird look. "What happened to *your* Jason Carter jersey?" he asked.

Juan had changed shirts. He now had on a Giants T-shirt.

"It's right here," Juan said. He slowly pulled his jersey from his book bag. "I want you to wear it," he said. He put the jersey in Marcus's lap.

Marcus's eyes lit up, and the gloomy look on his face turned to a smile. "For real?" he asked, hardly believing it. Marcus noticed a faint red spot on the front of the jersey. He could tell that Juan had tried to clean the ketchup stain.

"Sure," Juan said. "I had this Giants T-shirt in my book bag," he said, pointing at his chest.

"*Thanks, amigo,*" Marcus said, practicing his Spanish. "*Muchas gracias.*"

After that, Marcus talked the entire ride. "The way I see it, basketball is all I need," he said. "It will take me straight to the top, just like it did for Jason Carter."

"Yeah," Juan agreed. "And basketball will make us filthy rich!"

Marcus stared out the bus window daydreaming about Jason. "Did you know he wears a size-sixteen shoe?" he asked his best friend.

CHAPTER 4

"**W**e're here," Ms. Jordan told everyone as the bus crept into the parking lot.

"Yay!" they shouted.

"Line up next to your buddy," Ms. Jordan told the kids.

Everyone scrambled off the bus and formed two long lines.

Orange and dark blue flags, representing the team's colors, waved in the air high above the Dome where the Giants played.

Ms. Jordan walked next to Mia and her friend, Gabbie.

"Do you like basketball?" Ms. Jordan asked Mia.

"I like girls' basketball mostly," Mia said. "I would rather meet a women's basketball player like Lisa Smith or Rebecca Mathis. But meeting Jason Carter will be cool, too." Mia clutched the tape recorder close to her side. "I'm going to record everything he says," she told the teacher.

As they reached the front of the Dome, Marcus noticed a big banner that read: WELCOME TO GIANTS PRACTICE DAY!

A security guard greeted them and inspected their book bags. Then someone collected the bottom half of their tickets. Marcus stuck the other half of his ticket back into his pocket. He was going to keep it as a souvenir.

Inside the Dome, Ms. Jordan led them along a curving walkway. Marcus counted three popcorn stands before they reached an entrance to the bleachers.

"There must be a billion seats in here," Juan said, gazing at rows of bleachers that circled the shiny basketball court.

"Wow!" Marcus breathed, staring down at the court. It looked like the biggest court in the world. But he knew it was regulation size—the same as all the other professional basketball courts.

"Welcome to the home of the Giants!" a man screamed from the court in a friendly voice. He climbed up the steps to meet them. Curly locks of orange hair bounced as he moved.

"I've been expecting you," the man said. "I'm Rusty, the Giants tour guide."

"He sounds important," Mia whispered.

"When do we get to see the players?" Juan asked.

"You kids sure are lucky. Jason Carter is coming out to meet you before practice starts," Rusty said. "Right now all the players are in the locker room."

Marcus wondered how tall Jason's locker

was. And what was in it. He also wondered if Jason ever forgot the combination to his lock like Marcus sometimes did at school.

"Come on, follow me!" Rusty said. He dashed down the stairs.

The kids darted behind him.

When they got downstairs, Marcus took a closer look at the court. His gaze locked on the orange circle in the center. It looked like a giant basketball squished flat and tattooed on the wood. He imagined Jason standing there at tip-off with his hands reaching into the air, as if he were grasping for heaven. Then Marcus looked at the basketball goals. Each one looked so tiny. He imagined Jason swirling around like a ballerina and smashing the ball through the little rim all in the blink of an eye.

Rusty walked past the railing onto the court.

"Can we go out there?" Marcus asked.

"Of course," Rusty said, nodding.

"This is the best field trip ever," Marcus whispered to Juan. He hurried to the sidelines with the rest of his class. But he stopped just short of the court. With one more step, he would be standing on Jason Carter's turf. That was special territory.

Marcus took a deep breath and carefully placed his right foot down. *Screech!* The bottom of his Fly Carters let out a loud noise. The sound startled him. He quickly brought his left foot down before he lost his balance. *Screech!* the floor cried out again. Then the noise became louder and louder as pairs of his classmates' sneakers skidded onto the court.

The noise reminded Marcus of the squeaky-clean sound of glass cleaner being wiped off windows.

Finally the noise stopped, and everyone grew quiet. Marcus tiptoed to the center of the court. He could see his reflection in the floor.

It must have taken hours to polish these floors, he thought to himself. He wanted to dash to the free-throw line. But Marcus was scared to mess up the floor's sparkle. After all, his mother didn't let him slide around on their shiny dining room floor at home.

Bright lights suddenly beamed down on the court. Marcus knew that was his moment to shine. He quickly lifted his hands high in the air. His hands were grasping the ball he was saving for Jason Carter. Then Marcus imagined the crowd screaming his name. He raised up on the balls of his feet and stretched his body toward the basket. Just as Marcus was about to shoot the ball, he heard thundering footsteps.

"Who is that on my playground, ground, ground...?" a hollow voice cried out and echoed into the bleachers.

The deep voice startled the kids. Marcus wobbled on his tiptoes as he stood in perfect position to release his shot.

CHAPTER 5

The voice spoke again. "Just kidding ... I've been waiting to meet you. I'm Jason Carter," the voice echoed and disappeared. "Carter, Carter, Car ..."

Marcus's heart skipped a beat. He spun around like a soldier. Jason was standing so close, Marcus could touch him. Marcus dropped his head.

"Whoa!" he muttered, stepping back. The

biggest pair of Fly Carters he had ever seen was right in front of him. They made Marcus's sneakers look like baby shoes.

Trembling, Marcus looked up until he found Jason's face. He closed his eyes tight and opened them again.

He's a walking giant, Marcus thought to himself. "Awesome!" he mumbled under his breath.

Marcus opened his mouth to speak, but his voice left him. Finally, Marcus whispered, "Um, good afternoon, Mr. Carter."

"Speak up so Mr. Carter can hear you," Ms. Jordan said.

"Hello, Mr. Carter," everyone repeated in soft voices.

"What's up!" Jason said with a laugh. He pointed at Marcus's feet. "Hey, we're wearing the same shoes!"

Marcus flashed a smile. "I know," he said.

"Thanks for coming to Practice Day. It's going to be fun having you guys here to watch," Jason said. "Sit down and make yourselves comfortable." His tall body sank to the floor. Then he crossed his legs like a pretzel.

All the kids scrambled around him.

Screech! the floor cried out again as Marcus slid across it. He raced his classmates to a spot next to Jason. Marcus crossed his legs like a pretzel, too. He plopped the basketball in his lap.

Mia scooted close beside him. She carefully placed her tape recorder on the court. Then she pressed the record button to turn it on.

"Who all do we have here?" Jason asked. He looked over at Mia. "What's your name?"

"I'm Mia Robinson," she said.

"Nice to meet you, Mia," he said, reaching to shake her hand. Then he leaned over the tape recorder and said "Helloooo, helloooo, helloooo!"

The class laughed.

Jason sprang back up onto his feet. He made his way around the circle, and everyone introduced themselves. He met all of the kids and gave each one a firm handshake.

Marcus was the last one. "And who are you?" Jason asked, bending down in front of him.

His eyes met his hero's. "My name is Marcus."

The basketball player stretched his long arm toward Marcus. It dangled like a spaghetti noodle. Marcus noticed a ring on Jason's finger. It was a championship ring.

Marcus quickly put out his left hand. Wrong hand. He snatched it back. Finally, his right hand touched Jason's. They shook hands.

Jason squeezed Marcus's knuckles so tightly he thought they would crumble.

"So you want to hear about my job?" Jason asked as he sat back down.

"Yeah!" they shouted.

Ah, man, Marcus thought to himself. He wanted Jason to talk about basketball. He wanted to know how old Jason was when he first dunked the ball, his longest shot, and lots of other stuff about basketball. He didn't want to listen to him talk about a job.

"I love basketball!" Jason said. "Scoring the winning basket in front of thousands of screaming fans is one of the best feelings in the world. It sends tingles down my spine."

A smile grew on Marcus's face.

"I'm lucky to play with the Giants. Teamwork is our secret to winning," Jason said. "And winning has great rewards. When we won the championship, we got invited to the White House to meet the president. And my picture was on the cover of *Sports Illustrated*. My parents were very proud of me."

"Cool!" Marcus whispered to Juan.

"I wish special things like that happened every day," Jason said. "But most of my days are not that exciting. Actually, my job is often hard work. We practice quite a bit. Usually six days a week."

"That's a lot!" Juan said.

"And I always have to be here on time," Jason told them. "If I'm late, it costs me big bucks. I have to pay a one-thousand-dollar fine."

"One thousand dollars!" Rupert repeated.

"Whew!" the kids whispered.

Jason laughed. "Yep. That's a huge fine!

And that's why I'm never late," he said. "But I do more than just practice shooting hoops and play in games. I get up at six o'clock every morning and run three miles. Then I lift weights, study game tapes, and read stacks of playbooks. It's all part of my job."

Marcus raised his hand and waited for Jason to call on him.

"How long have you been a professional basketball player?" Marcus asked. He already knew the answer. But it was one of the questions his classmates told him to ask.

"Three years. I've been with the Giants since I finished college," Jason said. "My first game with the Giants was against the Cougars," he continued. "Johnny Pixley was the Cougar's star player. But he was my old teammate from college."

Jason laughed. "On the last play of the game, I suddenly forgot that Johnny and I didn't play on the same team anymore. I passed the ball to Johnny by mistake, and he blasted down the court and scored the winning basket for the Cougars."

Jason shook his head like he was trying to shake that story out of his mind. "After the game, my new teammates didn't speak to me for two days," Jason said. "That first week, I would have given anything to go back and play on my old college team."

"Where did you go to college?" Marcus asked.

"I graduated from good old Morehouse College," Jason said. "You know who Dr. Martin Luther King Jr. is, don't you?" he asked the class.

"Yes," the students replied.

"He graduated from Morehouse, too," Jason told the kids.

"And so did Johnny Pixley!" Juan teased.

Jason chuckled. "That's right," he said.

"Is that why you're wearing a Morehouse sweatshirt?" Mia asked.

Jason nodded his head. "I wore this same shirt before all of my games in college." He rubbed the front of his sweatshirt. "And for my tests, too. It brings me good luck."

Marcus saw that the letter *M* on Jason's sweatshirt was beginning to fade. And the shirt looked a little snug. Jason must have had it for a long time.

Suddenly, Marcus remembered his crumpled jersey at home. He wished he could have worn it as long as Jason has worn his sweatshirt. But he knew that was impossible. He sighed.

Then he checked out Jason from head to toe. Although his shirt was old, his Fly Carter sneakers looked brand-new. And that big ring on his finger kept flashing.

"Ask him my question," Juan whispered in Marcus's ear.

"With all the money you make, why did you go to college?" Marcus asked.

"I could have played pro ball as soon as I finished high school. A few coaches wanted me to join their teams," Jason said.

Then he tilted his head to one side and smiled as he gazed up. For a second, he looked as if his mind had drifted into the clouds. "I was thrilled! I had always dreamed of playing pro ball," he said. "But my parents and I had also dreamed about me going to college. I wanted to learn more about other things I liked. I'm really glad I did."

Marcus wondered what Jason's favorite class was.

Jason looked down at his reflection in the shiny wooden floor. "When I was your age, I loved to experiment," he said.

"You did?" Gabbie asked.

"Yep. One day, I had a craving for chocolate water," Jason said.

"Chocolate water?" Juan said with a giggle.

"Yes, chocolate water. I got tired of drinking chocolate milk. So, when my mom wasn't watching, I created my new drink," Jason said.

"How did it taste?" Gabbie asked.

"Gross!" Jason laughed.

"Did your mom get mad at you?" Mia asked.

"She wasn't happy," Jason said. "But I didn't get in trouble. Instead, she bought me a chemistry set."

"You mean you didn't spend all of your free time playing basketball?" Marcus asked.

"Nope," he said. "I loved basketball. But I spent lots of time playing with my friends and just doing normal kid things. And I used my chemistry set to make all kinds of con-coctions."

"You did?" Rupert asked.

"Sure. I even studied chemistry in college. It was my favorite class," he said.

Marcus tried to imagine Jason dressed in a white lab coat and goggles. He giggled quietly.

"Do you still have your chemistry set?" Mia asked.

"I don't think so," Jason said. "But I still might like to be a chemist some day."

"Why would you want to stop playing basketball to do chemistry?" Rupert asked.

"I could get hurt one day, like my teammate Cliff did," Jason said.

"Cliff Carlson?" Marcus asked. Marcus remembered his name from the Giants roster.

"Yes. Cliff was one of the best centers the Giants ever had. We called him Cliffhanger because he loved to hang from the basket when he dunked the ball," Jason said. "But he hurt his knee last season, and he'll probably never play professionally again."

Jason pulled his knee to his chest. "If that happened to me, I'd have to find something else to do," he said. "And even if it doesn't, I know I won't play basketball forever."

Jason stretched his leg out. "Ever seen an eighty-year-old basketball player?"

"No," the kids said, giggling.

Marcus winced. He couldn't imagine basketball without Jason Carter. As far as he knew, Jason had *invented* the slam dunk.

CHAPTER 6

Fans trickled into the stands.

Jason glanced at the clock on the scoreboard and stood up. "We've spent enough time talking about me," he said. "I want to hear about all of you."

Everyone grew quiet as they got up on their feet. Marcus crossed his arms tightly and frowned. He could listen to his classmates talk anytime. He wanted to hear more about Jason.

"What do you all want to be when you grow up?" Jason asked.

"A pilot," Gabbie said.

"I want to be a doctor," someone else said.

"I don't know," someone said.

"I'm going to be a news reporter," Mia announced.

"So that's why you're taping everything I say?" Jason asked, glancing at her tape recorder. Then he chuckled.

"Yes," Mia said. "I'm going to write a story about our field trip to see you."

"Will you promise to send me a copy?" Jason asked. "I'll even give it to my friend, Jay. We played basketball together in college. Now he's a reporter for a newspaper."

"Sure," Mia said, grinning. "I have my own newspaper, too," she added.

"You do?" Jason asked, sounding surprised.

Mia nodded. "It's called *Mia's World*," she said. "That's where I'm putting the story about you."

"That's great!" Jason said.

Marcus slowly swirled the basketball in the palm of one hand.

"I think I'll be a web designer or a nurse," someone else said.

"I like to draw," someone said. "Maybe I'll be an architect."

"My friend, Greg, is an architect," Jason said. "He designs all kinds of fancy buildings. When he was a kid, he designed his own tree house. It was the only one on our block with a basketball goal."

Lots of kids told Jason they wanted to be professional basketball and football players. Some told him they loved music, and they wanted to be pop singers, rock stars, or famous rappers.

Marcus's heart raced. He could hardly wait for Jason to call on him.

"And what about you?" Jason asked Marcus.

"I want to be a basketball player, just like you," Marcus told his hero.

CHAPTER 7

Jason suddenly stuck two fingers in his mouth and whistled.

Phhweeet!

The shrill sound was so loud Marcus nearly jumped out of his skin. Others covered their ears.

Jason jogged to the center of the circle. "All future ball players raise your hands," he announced with his hands on his hips. He sounded like a captain in the army.

Marcus, Juan, and four other boys waved their hands in the air. Tall, lanky Tammy Thomas raised hers, too.

Jason pointed at Marcus. The championship ring sparkled again. "Why do you want to play ball?" he asked.

Marcus looked puzzled. "Because I'm really good at it," he said.

Then Jason looked over at Juan. "And what about you?" he asked.

"I'm good, too," Juan said.

"Me, too," Tammy said, nibbling on a fingernail.

"I'm a great player," Rupert said. He sounded like he did when he tried to make Ms. Jordan believe he wasn't the one flying paper airplanes across the room.

"Lots of great players tried out for the Giants this year. But only four were picked,"

Jason told them. "What if you don't become a pro basketball player?"

Marcus shrugged his shoulders. "I don't know," he said in a soft voice.

Jason walked over to him.

Marcus looked up. "Basketball is the only thing I like to do—except math," he told Jason. "But I don't know what times tables and a bunch of fractions will ever do for me."

"You'd be surprised," Jason said. Then he turned to the stands behind him.

"See those chairs behind the computers?" Jason asked, pointing to the first row.

The kids looked over and nodded.

"A guy named Matt sits in the first chair at every game," Jason said. "He does the statistics for our team."

"He has a great seat," Juan whispered to Marcus.

"Matt keeps track of every shot I make

and every one I miss," Jason said. "He even uses math to figure out the statistics on my trading cards."

Marcus dug into his back pocket and slid something out. "You mean like this?" he asked, holding up a shiny, thin card. Jason's picture was on the front.

"Yes," Jason said, taking the card from Marcus's hand. He flipped it over and squinted to read the numbers on the back.

"Wow! I haven't looked at one of these in a while," he said. "It says I scored two thousand, three hundred twenty-one points last season." Then he passed the trading card around the circle so everyone could see it.

"And you blocked one hundred twenty-three shots," Marcus said. He had memorized all of Jason's stats.

"Sounds like someone knows a little bit about me," Jason said.

"He collects all of your trading cards," Mia said. "He gets them from boxes of cereal."

"You must know him pretty well," said Jason.

Marcus dropped his head and nervously tapped his foot. He hoped Jason hadn't noticed that Mia was taller than he was.

"I do. We're twins," Mia said. Then she smiled a sweet smile.

Marcus blushed. He wanted to turn away

and pretend he didn't know Mia. But he couldn't. He stared at the floor and said nothing.

"I thought you two looked alike," Jason said. "You guys sure are lucky."

Marcus jerked his head up and looked at Jason. "Why?" he asked.

"I always wanted a twin," Jason said with a grin.

Marcus breathed a deep sigh of relief.

CHAPTER

8

*B*uooounk! The buzzer blasted.

"That's the warning clock," Jason said. It's countdown time."

A Giants trainer rushed onto the court. "Sorry to interrupt you, Jason, but the practice game starts in fifteen minutes," he said.

"I'll be ready," he told the trainer.

Rusty waited to take the kids to their seats. Marcus noticed that Rusty was holding a Giants poster in his hands.

"Will you autograph a poster for the class before you leave?" Rusty asked Jason.

"Yeah!" the kids shouted. "Cool!"

"Sure," Jason said.

Rusty handed Jason the poster. Jason autographed it and gave it to Ms. Jordan.

"This is very special," Ms. Jordan said with a smile. "Class, what do you say to Mr. Carter?"

"Thank you, Mr. Carter," everyone said.

"You're very welcome," Jason said.

Ms. Jordan cleared her throat loudly and glared at Marcus.

Marcus was so excited he had almost forgotten. "Oh!" he said, raising his bushy eyebrows. He grabbed the basketball and scurried over to Jason.

"Uh," he mumbled. "Mr. Carter, our class has a special gift for you." Marcus spun the ball around. Then he stretched his arms out and presented it to Jason.

"This is for you," he said, sticking out his chest. "We all signed it."

Jason blushed. "Thank you, everybody. What a surprise," he said, inspecting the ball.

Marcus lifted his chin. "I got to give it to you because I won the math contest at school," he said in a low voice. Then he smiled a crooked smile.

"You really are good at math. Well, congratulations!" Jason said, smiling.

"Hold this for a second," he said, tossing the ball back to Marcus.

The ball wobbled as Marcus caught it.

"Quick!" Jason said, clapping his hands. "I need two kids to help me warm up."

Hands flew up. "Me! Me! No, me!" everyone shouted.

Jason called on Marcus and Mia. "I'll let double trouble help me today," he said with a laugh. Jason took off his sweatshirt and handed it to Mia. "Can you hold my lucky sweatshirt for me, please?" he asked her.

Mia gulped. "Sure," she said, carefully laying the shirt over her arm. "I'll take extra special care of it."

"Thanks," Jason said with a wink. Then he pointed at Marcus. "Pass me the ball, champ."

Wow, he called me "champ," Marcus thought to himself. He still wasn't sure if Jason had noticed that he was shorter than Mia. But it didn't matter because at that moment Marcus felt seven feet tall.

Marcus took a deep breath and rolled the ball between his sweaty palms. He lunged forward and threw it as hard as he could.

The Giants' star athlete flung his arm out and caught the ball with one hand. He jogged down the court bouncing the ball. He dribbled behind his back and blasted

into open court. Then he stepped back and did a crisscross dribble. He drove into the lane and leaped off the floor. His feet dangled in midair as he glided to the rim and slam-dunked the ball.

Swoosh! the net cried out. The backboard shook.

"Whoa!" the class whispered. Then they roared.

Jason called for everyone to line up behind the free-throw line. They hurried over and took turns shooting baskets.

Marcus and Mia went last because they were Jason's helpers.

Mia gave Jason's sweatshirt back to him just before she took her shot. "Two points," she shouted as she scored a basket.

"Dos!" Marcus screamed as he shot the ball. It sailed through the rim.

Then Marcus scooped up the ball. He

gazed around the court as if he were in a trance. His eyes shone. *I'll be back one day*, he said to himself. Then he gave the ball back to Jason.

The kids huddled in front of the basketball hero.

"Not bad," Jason told them as he reached for his basketball. "Keep practicing. But always dream more than one dream. And try to make all your dreams come true."

As he walked away, he looked back and said, "Then when you grow up, you can be anything you want to be. Now that's a *real* slam dunk."